WHITSTABLE
TRAVEL GUIDE 2025

Must-See Sights, Cozy Stays, and Insider Tips for an Unforgettable Escape

Julio Coder

COPYRIGHT © 2025 BY JULIO CODER

All rights reserved. Except for brief quotations included in critical reviews and certain other noncommercial uses allowed by copyright law, no part of this publication may be reproduced, distributed, or transmitted in any form or by any means, including photocopying, recording, or other electronic or mechanical methods, without the publisher's prior written permission.

TABLE OF CONTENTS

CHAPTER ONE: WELCOME TO WHITSTABLE

CHAPTER TWO: TOP ATTRACTIONS YOU CAN'T MISS

CHAPTER THREE: BEACHES, COASTAL WALKS, AND OUTDOOR FUN

CHAPTER FOUR: LOCAL FLAVORS AND FOODIE FINDS

CHAPTER FIVE: WHERE TO STAY: COZY STAYS AND UNIQUE ESCAPES

CHAPTER SIX: ART, CULTURE, AND CREATIVITY

CHAPTER SEVEN: SHOPPING AND LOCAL TREASURES

CHAPTER EIGHT: DAY TRIPS AND NEARBY ATTRACTIONS

CHAPTER NINE: INSIDER TIPS AND LOCAL ETIQUETTE

CHAPTER TEN: CONCLUSION: YOUR WHITSTABLE ADVENTURE AWAITS

CHAPTER ONE: WELCOME TO WHITSTABLE

Whitstable is a charming coastal town located in the county of Kent, England, renowned for its scenic landscapes, rich maritime history, and vibrant community spirit. Nestled along the northern coast of Kent, this quaint town boasts a mix of natural beauty, unique cultural heritage, and modern attractions. As Whitstable continues to evolve, it remains one of the most popular destinations for visitors seeking a coastal escape just an hour away from London.

A Brief History of Whitstable

Whitstable's history stretches back thousands of years, and the town's connection to the sea has shaped its development. Originally a small fishing village, Whitstable's location on the shores of the Thames Estuary provided the perfect base for maritime activities.

Prehistoric and Roman Times

The area around Whitstable has been inhabited for millennia, with evidence of human activity dating back to the prehistoric era. Archaeological discoveries suggest that early settlers were drawn to the area due to its proximity to the sea and the abundance of natural resources, including flint for tools and fishing opportunities.

During the Roman period, the town began to take on a more structured role in the region's economy. The Romans established a network of ports and settlements along the southeastern coast, and Whitstable likely served as one of these coastal outposts. While little physical evidence of Roman settlement remains in the town itself, nearby sites like the Roman fort at Reculver are a testament to the area's strategic importance.

The Rise of Whitstable as a Fishing Port

Whitstable's true maritime history began to take shape during the Middle Ages. By the 13th century, the town had become an important center for the fishing industry, particularly for the cultivation of oysters. Whitstable oysters gained a reputation for their quality, and the town's oyster beds became one of its primary sources of income. The town's history as an oyster port is still celebrated today, and Whitstable's oyster trade remains a central part of its identity.

During the 18th and 19th centuries, Whitstable's fishing industry flourished, with the town becoming known for its innovative approach to boat building. The introduction of the "Whitstable boat" in the early 19th century revolutionized the fishing industry by making it easier to catch oysters and other marine life.

Victorian Development and Tourism
In the late 19th century, Whitstable began to see growth in tourism. Its proximity to London made it an attractive destination for city dwellers seeking a coastal retreat. The construction of the Whitstable Railway in 1830 opened up easier

access to the town, and Whitstable quickly became known for its sandy beaches, quaint charm, and relaxing atmosphere.

The Victorians also played a significant role in shaping Whitstable's cultural identity. The town's iconic architecture, including the charming fishermen's cottages and the distinct Victorian terraced houses, still characterizes the town today. The Whitstable Hotel, originally built as a seaside retreat, continues to serve as one of the town's most prominent historic landmarks.

20th Century and Modern Growth
Throughout the 20th century, Whitstable maintained its status as a traditional seaside resort. In the 1950s and 1960s, it experienced a boom in popularity as a holiday destination, particularly for Londoners looking for a weekend escape. While the fishing industry continued to play an important role, Whitstable's reputation as a coastal getaway began to grow alongside its development as an artistic hub.

In recent decades, Whitstable has undergone significant gentrification. Artists and creative professionals, drawn by the town's beauty and sense of community, have settled here, contributing to the town's growing reputation as a cultural center. The arrival of boutique shops, contemporary art galleries, and artisan cafes has given Whitstable a more modern and cosmopolitan feel, while still preserving its historic charm.

Today, Whitstable is a vibrant community that draws visitors year-round for its blend of tradition, art, culture, and natural beauty.

Why Visit Whitstable in 2025?
Whitstable has something to offer every type of traveler, from history enthusiasts and foodies to nature lovers and culture seekers. Here's why Whitstable should be on your list of must-visit destinations in 2025:

1. A Coastal Escape Near London

For city dwellers looking to escape the hustle and bustle of London, Whitstable is the perfect coastal retreat. With its easy access from the capital—just over an hour by train—it's an ideal spot for a weekend getaway. Whether you're visiting for a few hours or planning a longer stay, Whitstable offers a serene setting that is just far enough from the city to feel like a true escape.

2. Unmatched Oysters and Seafood

Whitstable's oysters are legendary, and the town remains one of the top spots in the UK to sample this iconic shellfish. The Whitstable Oyster Festival, held annually in late July, is a must-visit event for food lovers, where you can taste freshly shucked oysters, indulge in seafood delicacies, and enjoy live music and festivities. The town's seafood restaurants, including the popular Wheelers Oyster Bar, continue to serve up delicious catches from the local waters.

Aside from oysters, Whitstable is known for its excellent selection of seafood, from fresh fish and crab to other shellfish. Whether you're dining at a Michelin-starred restaurant or enjoying a casual meal at a fish and chip shop, Whitstable offers an unparalleled seafood experience.

3. Vibrant Arts and Culture Scene
Whitstable has long been an artistic haven. In 2025, the town continues to support a thriving creative community. The Whitstable Biennale, a celebration of contemporary visual art, is one of the key cultural events that draws artists and visitors from all over the world. The town is also home to a range of art galleries, including the Whitstable Art Gallery and the Harbour Gallery, where visitors can explore everything from painting and sculpture to photography and digital art.

For those who appreciate music, the town hosts a variety of events throughout the year, including the Whitstable Music Festival. The mix of cultural offerings makes Whitstable an ideal destination for those seeking an artsy and creative atmosphere.

4. Natural Beauty and Outdoor Activities
Whitstable is not only known for its lively town center but also its stunning natural surroundings. The town is blessed with a beautiful coastline, where you can take leisurely walks along the beach, cycle through picturesque countryside, or enjoy birdwatching at nearby nature reserves. The nearby Herne Bay and Tankerton Slopes offer more scenic views and opportunities for outdoor exploration.

For walkers and hikers, the surrounding Kent countryside provides plenty of trails, including the popular Viking Coastal Trail, which offers stunning views of the sea and the surrounding landscapes. In 2025, these outdoor experiences continue to attract nature enthusiasts and outdoor adventurers.

5. Historic Landmarks and Heritage

Whitstable's rich history is still visible throughout the town, with numerous landmarks that tell the story of its maritime past. Whitstable Harbour, a working port that still sees activity today, is a great spot for a relaxing stroll and offers insight into the town's fishing heritage. Other notable historical sites include the Whitstable Castle, a Victorian-era castle surrounded by beautiful gardens, and the Whitstable Museum, which houses artifacts and exhibits related to the town's history.

In 2025, the town's historical charm remains intact, making it an excellent destination for those interested in learning about Whitstable's past.

How to Get There and Around
Whitstable's location on the southeast coast of England makes it easily accessible by train, car, or bus, and there are plenty of options for getting around once you arrive.

1. By Train

One of the easiest ways to reach Whitstable is by train. Whitstable is served by the Whitstable Railway Station, which connects the town to London and other major towns along the southeast coast. The journey from London's Victoria Station to Whitstable takes around 1 hour and 10 minutes, making it a convenient option for day trips or weekend breaks. Trains run frequently throughout the day, and the station is located just a short walk from the town center and the beach.

2. By Car

For those who prefer to drive, Whitstable is well connected by road. The town is accessible via the A299, which links to the M2 motorway and provides easy access from London, Canterbury, and other nearby towns. The drive from London takes approximately 1 hour and 30 minutes, depending on traffic conditions. Once in Whitstable, there are several car parks available, including those near the beach and town center.

3. By Bus

If you're traveling by bus, Whitstable is well served by local and regional bus routes. The main bus station is located in the town center, and services connect Whitstable with nearby towns like Canterbury, Herne Bay, and Faversham. You can also take a coach from London, though the journey may take longer compared to the train.

4. Getting Around Whitstable

Once in Whitstable, the town is easily navigable on foot. The town center, including its shops, restaurants, and beach, is compact, so it's easy to explore on foot. Bicycles are also a popular mode of transport, and bike rental shops are available if you want to cycle along the coastline or through the surrounding countryside.

For those looking to explore the wider area, buses and taxis are readily available. The local bus services connect Whitstable to neighboring towns, while taxis can be hailed or pre-booked for more convenience.

Whitstable's charm, history, and modern attractions make it an ideal destination for visitors in 2025. Whether you're drawn by its maritime heritage, vibrant arts scene, or natural beauty, the town promises an unforgettable experience.

CHAPTER TWO: TOP ATTRACTIONS YOU CAN'T MISS

Whitstable Harbour and Harbour Market

Whitstable Harbour is the heart of the town's maritime heritage, where visitors can experience the ongoing traditions of the local fishing industry while enjoying the vibrant atmosphere of the surrounding area. The harbour itself, originally established as a small port for local fishermen, has been a key part of Whitstable's economy for centuries, and it continues to be a working port today.

History and Significance

Whitstable Harbour has deep historical roots, with its origins stretching back to the 13th century when it first began to operate as a port for fishing boats. In the 19th century, the harbour underwent significant improvements to support the growing demand for oyster harvesting, one of Whitstable's most famous exports. The iconic Whitstable oyster trade became so vital to the local economy that the town was eventually granted its own pier in the 1830s to accommodate the thriving seafood trade.

Today, the Harbour is not only home to an active fishing fleet, but it also serves as a gateway for leisure activities such as boating and water sports. While the commercial boats still operate out of the harbour, visitors will often see smaller pleasure crafts, providing a more relaxed and picturesque environment compared to other commercial harbours.

The Harbour Market
The Harbour Market, located in the heart of Whitstable Harbour, is a bustling hub of local goods, artisan products, and street food. It is one of the most popular places to visit in Whitstable and offers a diverse selection of stalls selling everything from handmade crafts to fresh produce, artisan cheeses, and locally sourced seafood. This market has become an essential

part of Whitstable's community, blending the town's rich fishing history with its contemporary artistic and culinary culture.

Each weekend, visitors can stroll through the market and sample delicacies such as smoked fish, homemade baked goods, and local fruits and vegetables. The Harbour Market is also known for its vibrant arts and crafts stalls, where you can purchase unique pieces from local artists and craftspeople. These include pottery, jewelry, textiles, and paintings inspired by the coastal landscape.

As you wander through the market, you'll encounter local chefs offering fresh dishes prepared on-site, and the atmosphere is often lively with live music performances or other events throughout the year. It's the perfect spot for lunch, a casual drink, or picking up a souvenir that reflects the town's local culture and character.

The Famous Oyster Experience

Whitstable is synonymous with oysters, and the town's oyster industry continues to be a significant part of its identity. The history of oyster farming in Whitstable dates back to at least the 14th century, and the Whitstable Oyster Company still operates in the area today, producing some of the finest oysters in the country. For visitors to the town, experiencing Whitstable's oysters is a must-do.

Oyster Festivals and Events

The Whitstable Oyster Festival, which takes place every summer, is one of the biggest events of the year, attracting foodies, history enthusiasts, and locals alike. Originally a celebration of the oyster harvest, the festival has evolved into a week-long celebration of Whitstable's maritime heritage. The festival typically includes oyster shucking competitions, oyster-eating contests, live music, parades, and street food stalls. It's an exciting time for visitors to experience the town's famous oysters in a fun and lively atmosphere.

Throughout the year, various local seafood restaurants and bars offer a taste of Whitstable's oysters, but the festival is an especially exciting time to enjoy the fresh seafood in the company of like-minded food enthusiasts.

Oyster Tasting and Farm Tours
For those interested in learning more about the oyster industry, several local businesses offer guided tours of Whitstable's oyster farms. These tours provide a fascinating behind-the-scenes look at how oysters are farmed, harvested, and prepared for sale. Many of the tours include a tasting session, where visitors can sample a selection of freshly shucked oysters, often accompanied by a glass of local champagne or white wine.

The most popular spots to try oysters include famous establishments like Wheelers Oyster Bar, which has been serving Whitstable oysters for over 160 years, and The Lobster Shack, known for its variety of seafood dishes, including oysters served in various styles. The experience often includes pairing oysters with locally sourced accompaniments such as mignonette sauce, fresh lemon, and horseradish. Whether raw, smoked, or cooked, Whitstable oysters provide an unforgettable tasting experience that can be paired with a relaxing day by the coast.

Whitstable Castle and Gardens

Another key attraction in Whitstable is Whitstable Castle, a Grade II-listed building that serves as both a historical landmark and a popular visitor destination. Located just outside the main town center, Whitstable Castle offers not only a rich history but also beautiful gardens, making it a great place for a relaxing stroll or a picnic.

History and Architecture

Whitstable Castle was built in 1792 as a private residence for the influential local landowner, Sir Thomas and Lady Finch-Hatton. Initially designed in the style of a small Gothic country house, it later underwent significant renovations in the Victorian era. The castle's architecture reflects a mix of Gothic and Tudor revival styles, with intricate stonework, pointed windows, and a steeply pitched roof. Over the years, the castle passed through various hands and was eventually opened to the public in the mid-20th century.

The castle's historical significance lies not only in its architectural beauty but also in its connection to Whitstable's development. It was built during a period of growing interest in Whitstable as a coastal retreat for the wealthy, and it stands as a reminder of the town's emergence as a fashionable seaside resort.

Gardens and Grounds
The gardens surrounding Whitstable Castle are as much of an attraction as the building itself. Spanning over 5 acres, the gardens feature a mix of formal landscaping and natural woodland, providing a tranquil escape from the more commercial areas of Whitstable. Visitors can explore the well-maintained lawns, rose gardens,

and exotic plants that create a peaceful environment for relaxation or contemplation.

The Castle Grounds are also home to a café, which offers a selection of homemade cakes, light snacks, and refreshments. It's an ideal spot to relax after a stroll through the gardens or a visit to the castle's historical rooms. For those visiting with children, the playground in the castle grounds is a popular option for family-friendly enjoyment.

The Castle and Community Events
Throughout the year, Whitstable Castle hosts a variety of events that showcase the town's vibrant community spirit. These include live music performances, art exhibitions, and community festivals. In 2025, the castle's events calendar is set to feature a mix of cultural activities such as Shakespearean plays in the gardens, classical music concerts, and seasonal outdoor markets. These events make Whitstable Castle an exciting and dynamic part of the town's cultural life.

The castle is also available for private events and weddings, adding to its status as a prime local venue. With its stunning architecture, beautiful gardens, and historical significance, Whitstable Castle is a must-visit attraction for anyone interested in the town's past, present, and future.

Conclusion

Whitstable offers a variety of attractions that cater to all types of visitors, whether you're a food lover, history buff, or nature enthusiast. The Whitstable Harbour, with its lively market and ongoing maritime traditions, remains a central hub for the town's community. The famous oysters, which have put Whitstable on the map as a culinary destination, offer an unparalleled taste of the town's rich maritime history. Whitstable Castle, with its charming architecture and peaceful gardens, provides a serene escape that highlights both the town's past and its present-day cultural vibrancy.

CHAPTER THREE: BEACHES, COASTAL WALKS, AND OUTDOOR FUN

Tankerton Slopes and Beach Huts

Tankerton Slopes is one of Whitstable's most iconic outdoor destinations, offering an ideal blend of scenic views, historical significance, and a laid-back atmosphere. Stretching along the coastline, Tankerton Slopes offers a wide, gently sloping grassy hill that leads down to the pebble beach, with expansive views over the Thames Estuary. The area is popular among both locals and visitors, who come to relax, enjoy outdoor activities, or simply take in the stunning coastal vistas.

Tankerton Slopes: History and Landscape

Tankerton Slopes has a rich history that ties into the development of Whitstable as a seaside resort during the 19th century. Originally, the area was a natural piece of coastal land, but as

Whitstable became more popular with tourists in the Victorian era, the slopes were landscaped and developed for leisure activities. Tankerton Slopes continues to be one of the best-preserved examples of Whitstable's heritage as a coastal retreat, maintaining much of its original charm.

The slopes themselves are a haven for nature lovers, with a variety of native flora and fauna to discover, especially during the warmer months. The area is also home to a wide range of wildflowers, making it an excellent spot for casual walks, picnics, or simply enjoying the peaceful surroundings. The open spaces and panoramic views over the sea make Tankerton Slopes a prime location for kite flying and other light outdoor activities.

Beach Huts: A Whitstable Tradition
One of the most striking features of Tankerton Slopes is the line of brightly colored beach huts that dot the landscape. These iconic structures are a quintessential part of the Whitstable experience. The beach huts, which have been a

tradition since the early 20th century, are not just functional but have become part of the town's social fabric, offering a place for families to store their beach gear or simply enjoy the views in a private setting.

In 2025, the beach huts remain an essential part of Tankerton Slopes, with many of them available for rent during the summer months. These small, brightly colored huts have become symbols of Whitstable's relaxed, family-friendly atmosphere. They are perfect for storing belongings while you take in the sea breeze, or for enjoying a quiet lunch overlooking the water.

The beach huts are often used by families, and the area around them is popular for sunbathing, beach games, and socializing. Whether you are visiting for a day at the beach or just to enjoy the coastal beauty, Tankerton Slopes and its beach huts provide the perfect setting for a relaxing outdoor experience.

Activities at Tankerton Slopes

Tankerton Slopes offers a variety of outdoor activities, making it an ideal destination for people of all ages. The gentle slope is perfect for families with young children, as it provides a safe area for picnics and play without the hazards of rough terrain. For those who enjoy a more active outdoor experience, the slopes provide ample space for kite flying, frisbee, or even informal ball games.

Cycling is another popular activity at Tankerton Slopes. The wide open spaces make it an excellent location for leisurely bike rides with a view, and the area is well-served by bike hire shops, making it easy for visitors to rent bikes for a day. Additionally, the slopes are a great starting point for more extended cycling adventures along the coastline.

The Crab and Winkle Way
The Crab and Winkle Way is a scenic 7.5-mile (12 km) cycle and walking trail that connects Whitstable to the historic city of Canterbury. This route follows the path of the former Crab

and Winkle Line, a railway that once ran between the two locations and was one of the first railways in the world to carry both passengers and freight, including Whitstable's famous oysters.

History of the Crab and Winkle Line
The Crab and Winkle Line, which opened in 1830, was one of the first railways to use steam locomotives to transport both people and goods. The line connected Whitstable with Canterbury, which helped to fuel the town's growth as a seaside resort by providing quick and easy access for visitors from the city. The railway was also crucial for transporting oysters from Whitstable's busy port to London and other major cities, further cementing the town's reputation as an oyster haven.

Though the line was closed to passengers in the 1950s and freight operations ceased shortly thereafter, the railway's legacy lives on through the Crab and Winkle Way, which follows much of the original route. Today, the trail is one of the best ways to explore the countryside surrounding Whitstable while learning about the area's railway history.

Walking and Cycling the Crab and Winkle Way

The Crab and Winkle Way is a well-maintained path suitable for both walking and cycling. Starting in the heart of Whitstable, the trail leads through peaceful countryside, passing through woodlands, meadows, and quiet rural roads. As you journey along the route, you'll encounter several picturesque villages and stunning views of the surrounding Kent countryside. Along the way, there are plenty of opportunities for a rest, with benches and picnic areas offering the perfect spots to relax and enjoy the scenery.

The path also passes several historical landmarks, including the medieval town of Canterbury, which is known for its UNESCO World Heritage-listed Cathedral and its rich history dating back to Roman times. For those interested in local history, the Crab and Winkle

Way offers a wealth of stories and sites to explore.

While the trail itself is relatively easy to walk, some sections can be quite hilly, making it more challenging for cyclists. However, those willing to take on the incline will be rewarded with breathtaking views of the countryside and the sea. Whether you're an avid cyclist or simply someone looking for a peaceful walk, the Crab and Winkle Way is an ideal way to experience the natural beauty and rich history of the area.

Highlights of the Trail

Whitstable: Starting at the harbor, the trail provides an excellent introduction to Whitstable's lively atmosphere, its beach huts, and its coastal beauty.
The Creek: As you leave Whitstable behind, you'll pass through areas of natural beauty like the Horsebridge Recreation Ground, which offers scenic views of the surrounding countryside.

The Canterbury Landscape: As you approach Canterbury, the path leads through quiet woodlands and lush meadows. You'll also cross some of the famous "Wool Churches" that dot the Kentish landscape, offering a glimpse of the region's rural heritage.

Canterbury: The end of the trail brings you to the historic city of Canterbury, where the Cathedral is the centerpiece of the town's medieval layout. The walk is a perfect way to combine natural beauty with historical exploration.

Sailing, Kayaking, and Paddleboarding

Whitstable's location on the Thames Estuary makes it an ideal destination for water sports and outdoor activities. The town's beaches and calm, shallow waters provide the perfect conditions for a variety of activities, from sailing to kayaking to paddleboarding.

Sailing in Whitstable

Whitstable is known for its excellent sailing conditions, thanks to its protected waters and consistent winds. The town has a long tradition of sailing, dating back to the 19th century when it was a center for oyster dredging and fishing. Today, sailing is a popular activity, with numerous sailing clubs, schools, and rental services available for both beginners and experienced sailors.

The Whitstable Yacht Club, established in 1880, is one of the key institutions in the local sailing scene, offering sailing courses, races, and a vibrant community for sailing enthusiasts. The club hosts regular sailing events throughout the year, and it is one of the best places to get involved in the local sailing culture. In addition, Whitstable Harbour serves as a launching point for sailors looking to explore the estuary, making it a convenient spot to start your sailing adventure.

For those new to sailing, there are plenty of opportunities for tuition and guided tours, offering a safe and enjoyable introduction to the sport. Whether you want to take a leisurely sail around the estuary or participate in a race, Whitstable offers a variety of options for sailors of all skill levels.

Kayaking and Paddleboarding
Kayaking and paddleboarding are also incredibly popular in Whitstable, offering a more relaxed way to enjoy the sea and explore the local coastline. The calm waters of the Thames Estuary make it a safe environment for beginners to try out these water sports. For those seeking an adrenaline rush, the estuary's tidal movements provide enough challenge to keep things interesting.

Several local businesses offer kayak and paddleboard rentals, as well as guided tours. Paddleboarding, in particular, has become a favorite among both locals and visitors, with its easy-to-learn nature and unique ability to connect with the water in a peaceful, serene manner. Many of the tours offer the chance to explore hidden coves, observe local wildlife, or enjoy a tranquil paddle along the shoreline, making it an unforgettable way to experience Whitstable's natural beauty.

Wildlife Watching from the Water
One of the added benefits of kayaking and paddleboarding in Whitstable is the opportunity to spot local wildlife. The Thames Estuary is home to a wide variety of birds, including migratory species that stop off along the coast. Birdwatchers often take to the water to observe species such as ospreys, herons, and various shorebirds, while kayakers and paddleboarders may also encounter seals and other marine life along the shoreline.

With the gentle flow of the estuary and the quiet serenity of the water, these activities offer a unique perspective on the coastal environment of Whitstable, and they are a perfect way to experience nature at a slower pace.

Conclusion
Whitstable offers a diverse range of outdoor activities that cater to all types of adventurers,

from those looking for a relaxing day at the beach to those seeking more active pursuits like cycling, sailing, or water sports. Tankerton Slopes, with its scenic views and beach huts, is a perfect place to unwind and enjoy the coastline. The Crab and Winkle Way provides an immersive experience in both the countryside and history, while sailing, kayaking, and paddleboarding offer unique opportunities to connect with Whitstable's stunning natural beauty. Each of these activities allows visitors to experience the charm and tranquility of this coastal town in different, memorable ways.

CHAPTER FOUR: LOCAL FLAVORS AND FOODIE FINDS

Seafood Hotspots and Oyster Bars

Whitstable has long been known for its abundant supply of fresh seafood, and the town's reputation for oysters, in particular, continues to make it a must-visit destination for food lovers. The town's location on the Thames Estuary, combined with its rich maritime heritage, makes it the ideal place to indulge in locally caught seafood, with a strong emphasis on oysters. Visitors can find a variety of seafood dining options that serve up the freshest catches of the day, from classic fish and chips to fine dining experiences featuring locally sourced shellfish.

Whitstable's Famous Oysters

Whitstable oysters are some of the finest in the UK, and the town's oyster bars and seafood restaurants have been serving them since the

14th century. Known for their sweet, delicate flavor and smooth texture, Whitstable oysters are often enjoyed raw on the half shell with a squeeze of lemon or a dash of mignonette sauce. The oysters in Whitstable are farmed in the Thames Estuary, where the combination of clean, nutrient-rich waters and the right conditions for oyster farming has created the perfect environment for producing this world-renowned delicacy.

Several restaurants and bars in Whitstable specialize in oysters, and they often serve them fresh from the sea with simple accompaniments. Many of these establishments offer a variety of oysters to choose from, including native oysters (Ostrea edulis) and the more commonly available Pacific oysters (Crassostrea gigas).

Popular Seafood Hotspots

1. Wheelers Oyster Bar
Wheelers Oyster Bar is one of Whitstable's most famous seafood restaurants, known for its long

history and its focus on fresh, local oysters. Established in 1856, Wheelers serves a range of oyster dishes, from the classic raw oysters to grilled versions and oyster stew. The intimate, unpretentious atmosphere makes it a popular choice among locals and visitors alike. This family-run establishment offers not only oysters but also a selection of fresh fish dishes, making it an essential stop for anyone looking to enjoy Whitstable's seafood.

2. The Lobster Shack
For a more casual yet equally delicious seafood experience, The Lobster Shack on the beach is a must-visit. Specializing in fresh seafood, particularly lobsters and oysters, The Lobster Shack serves up a variety of dishes in a laid-back, beachside setting. Patrons can enjoy their oysters raw, smoked, or in a variety of prepared dishes, all while taking in stunning views of the sea. The Lobster Shack is perfect for those looking to enjoy fresh seafood with a view.

3. Harbour Street Oyster Bar

Located near Whitstable Harbour, the Harbour Street Oyster Bar offers an exceptional selection of oysters and other shellfish. The menu here features oysters prepared in various ways, as well as seafood platters and daily specials that highlight the catch of the day. The small, cozy atmosphere of the restaurant allows for an intimate dining experience, making it an excellent choice for oyster lovers.

4. The Seasalter

Located just outside of Whitstable, The Seasalter is another seafood destination that draws visitors for its emphasis on fresh, local ingredients. While not exclusively an oyster bar, The Seasalter offers a range of seafood dishes, including a selection of oysters, alongside other fresh catches. The restaurant's menu changes seasonally, ensuring that diners always get the best of what's available.

The Oyster Experience

baked cakes, pastries, and snacks, making it a great stop for a mid-morning treat.

3. Gyllyngdune Café

Located in the Gyllyngdune Gardens, Gyllyngdune Café is an excellent spot to enjoy a peaceful coffee while surrounded by lush greenery. This charming café offers a range of hot drinks, sandwiches, and light bites, all made with locally sourced ingredients. The café's relaxed atmosphere makes it a perfect place to unwind after a walk through the nearby gardens.

Artisan Bakeries

1. The Real Bread Company

The Real Bread Company is a beloved local bakery in Whitstable, known for its handmade, artisanal bread. Using traditional baking methods and high-quality ingredients, The Real Bread Company offers a variety of freshly baked loaves, including sourdough, ciabatta, and multigrain bread. The bakery also sells pastries, cakes, and other baked goods, making it a great place to stop for a breakfast or a snack.

2. Suffolk Bakery

Suffolk Bakery offers a wide selection of freshly baked bread, pastries, cakes, and sweet treats. With a focus on quality and sustainability, Suffolk Bakery uses local ingredients whenever possible, ensuring that all of its products are fresh and full of flavor. Their croissants and homemade jams are particularly popular, making this bakery an essential stop for anyone looking for a breakfast or afternoon tea treat.

3. The Cake Shed

The Cake Shed is an independent bakery in Whitstable that specializes in homemade cakes, cookies, and pastries. Known for its indulgent offerings, The Cake Shed serves up an array of sweet treats, including cakes made with seasonal fruits, scones, and decadent brownies. Whether you're craving a classic Victoria sponge or something a bit more adventurous, The Cake Shed offers something for every sweet tooth.

Farmers' Markets and Food Festivals

Whitstable's commitment to local, sustainable food is evident in the town's thriving farmers' markets and food festivals. These events offer visitors the chance to sample some of the best produce, artisanal goods, and culinary delights the region has to offer. Whether you're looking for fresh fruit and vegetables, handmade cheeses, or specialty food items, the farmers' markets in Whitstable are an excellent way to taste the local flavors and meet the people who produce them.

Whitstable Farmers' Market

The Whitstable Farmers' Market, held regularly at the Whitstable Community Centre, is one of the best places to find locally grown produce, freshly baked bread, and artisanal food products. The market offers a wide range of seasonal fruits and vegetables, as well as handmade cheeses, cured meats, preserves, and locally produced honey. In addition to the food stalls, the market also features local artisans selling handmade goods, including pottery, jewelry, and textiles.

The farmers' market is a great place to pick up ingredients for a picnic or take home some unique food products that reflect the best of the Kent countryside. The market is also a great opportunity to chat with local producers, learn more about their methods, and discover new foods you may not find elsewhere.

Whitstable Oyster Festival
The Whitstable Oyster Festival is one of the town's most famous food-related events, celebrating the local oyster industry and the town's maritime heritage. Held every July, the festival includes a range of activities, from oyster shucking competitions and tastings to live music and food stalls. It is an excellent opportunity to sample a variety of local oysters and enjoy the lively atmosphere of the town as it celebrates its seafood culture.

During the festival, visitors can taste oysters in many different ways, from raw and smoked to grilled or deep-fried. There are also plenty of other seafood dishes to enjoy, as well as locally sourced wines, beers, and ciders. The festival provides a chance to not only enjoy the food but also learn more about the history of Whitstable's oyster industry, which has been vital to the town for centuries.

Kent Food and Drink Festival

The Kent Food and Drink Festival is another major event that celebrates the region's rich culinary offerings. Held annually in Canterbury, the festival showcases the best local produce, from fresh fruits and vegetables to artisanal cheeses and meats. The event features cooking demonstrations, tastings, and food stalls, allowing visitors to sample the region's finest food and drink products. For those staying in Whitstable, this festival provides an excellent opportunity to explore Kent's food scene beyond the town.

Conclusion

Whitstable's culinary scene is a testament to the town's rich history, its proximity to the sea, and its commitment to using local, sustainable ingredients. Whether you're indulging in the town's famous oysters, enjoying a relaxing coffee in a local café, or exploring the town's farmers' markets and food festivals, Whitstable offers a wide range of flavors that cater to all tastes. The town's food scene continues to evolve, but it remains rooted in its traditions, ensuring that visitors can enjoy the best of Kent's culinary heritage while experiencing all the charm Whitstable has to offer.

CHAPTER FIVE: WHERE TO STAY: COZY STAYS AND UNIQUE ESCAPES

Boutique Hotels and Inns

Whitstable's boutique hotels and inns provide an exceptional mix of comfort, charm, and personalized service, often in historic buildings or beautifully renovated spaces. These accommodations offer guests a more intimate and unique stay compared to the larger chains, with an emphasis on local character, design, and the surrounding coastal beauty.

1. The Crescent Turner Hotel

Situated just a short distance from Whitstable town center, the Crescent Turner Hotel offers a boutique experience in a charming, period building. The hotel features contemporary decor combined with historic features, providing guests with a stylish yet comfortable retreat. The rooms are equipped with modern amenities, including plush bedding, stylish furniture, and scenic views of the surrounding countryside. Many rooms have balconies or terraces, making it ideal for enjoying Whitstable's beautiful sunsets.

The hotel also features an on-site restaurant and bar, serving a menu inspired by the best local produce. The proximity to both the town and nearby nature reserves makes the Crescent Turner Hotel a perfect place for those looking to balance relaxation with exploring the outdoors. The small size and attentive service ensure a more personalized stay.

2. The Marine Hotel
The Marine Hotel is a popular boutique hotel situated along the seafront with stunning views of the Thames Estuary. Its history dates back to the Victorian era, and it retains much of its original character, blended with modern touches. The hotel offers a variety of rooms, from those with views of the sea to more secluded, cozy spaces ideal for a quiet stay.

Known for its exceptional location, The Marine Hotel is within walking distance of Whitstable's main attractions, including the harbor and the famous oyster bars. The on-site restaurant serves up fresh seafood, offering guests an authentic taste of Whitstable's culinary offerings. The relaxed atmosphere and elegant rooms make it a great choice for those looking for a refined yet welcoming escape.

3. The Hotel Continental

Located directly on Whitstable's seafront, The Hotel Continental is another excellent choice for boutique-style accommodation. This Victorian building has been lovingly restored and now offers a modern take on classic seaside hotel luxury. Each room is thoughtfully decorated, blending contemporary furnishings with traditional seaside elements. Many rooms boast spectacular views of the sea or the quaint surrounding streets of Whitstable.

The hotel features an impressive restaurant and bar, specializing in fresh, locally sourced ingredients. The atmosphere is warm and friendly, and the service is exceptional, with a focus on making every guest feel at home. The Hotel Continental's prime location near the beach and the bustling harbor area makes it ideal for exploring Whitstable while enjoying the comfort of a boutique hotel.

4. The Whitstable Hotel
Another top boutique hotel in Whitstable is The Whitstable Hotel, a chic and modern property located right on the seafront. Known for its minimalist design and luxurious finish, The Whitstable Hotel is perfect for those looking for a modern coastal retreat. Rooms feature clean lines, contemporary furniture, and beautiful views of the sea or the town.

The on-site restaurant serves a mix of traditional British and international cuisine, prepared with locally sourced ingredients. The hotel's stylish decor, modern amenities, and prime location make it a top choice for couples or solo travelers looking for a stylish and peaceful stay in Whitstable.

5. The Oyster Pearl Hotel

Located near Whitstable's bustling harbor area, The Oyster Pearl Hotel combines contemporary elegance with the charm of the town's maritime history. This boutique hotel offers a selection of beautifully designed rooms with a modern coastal theme. The property offers amenities such as a boutique shop, an in-house café serving delicious pastries, and a cozy lounge area where guests can unwind.

The Oyster Pearl Hotel is ideal for those looking to stay near the harbor and enjoy both the town's vibrant atmosphere and the peace of a well-designed retreat. The hotel's focus on local design elements and a personalized guest experience makes it a standout choice for boutique accommodations in Whitstable.

Beachfront Rentals and Cottages

For visitors seeking a more private and home-like experience, Whitstable offers a variety of beachfront rentals and cozy cottages. These properties allow guests to enjoy the coastal beauty of Whitstable while having the flexibility and comfort of home.

1. Seaside Cottage

Seaside Cottage offers a charming, cozy retreat just a short walk from Whitstable's beach. This traditional Victorian cottage has been beautifully restored and features a range of original features, such as exposed wooden beams and fireplaces, combined with modern comforts. The cottage has a well-equipped kitchen, making it ideal for those who prefer to cook their own meals using local ingredients.

The location is perfect for exploring Whitstable's beaches and nearby attractions, and the cottage is well-suited for small families or groups of friends. The peaceful surroundings and welcoming atmosphere make Seaside Cottage an excellent choice for a relaxing getaway.

2. Harbour House

Harbour House is a spacious, elegant property located directly by Whitstable Harbour, offering guests spectacular views of the boats and the estuary. This two-story house is beautifully furnished, with a large, open-plan living area, a modern kitchen, and multiple bedrooms to accommodate larger groups or families. The house is fully equipped for self-catering and provides a great balance between home comforts and luxurious amenities.

The location is ideal for exploring Whitstable on foot, as it is within walking distance of the beach, the town center, and the harbor. Harbour House is perfect for visitors who want a central base with access to everything Whitstable has to offer while still enjoying the tranquility of a beachfront location.

3. Beachside Retreat

For those who wish to be closer to nature, the Beachside Retreat offers a modern, stylish option just steps from the shoreline. This well-designed rental offers open-plan living with large windows that let in natural light and provide beautiful views of the sea. The interior combines contemporary decor with cozy touches, creating a welcoming space that feels like a true retreat.

The Beachside Retreat is a wonderful option for couples or small families looking for a quiet, intimate escape by the sea. The rental is equipped with everything you need for a comfortable stay, including a full kitchen, stylish living areas, and private outdoor space for enjoying the sea breeze.

4. Coastal Cottage
The Coastal Cottage offers a more rustic experience while still providing all the modern amenities that guests expect. Located on the outskirts of Whitstable, this cozy cottage has been fully renovated to provide a comfortable,

private escape with a focus on sustainable living. The property offers a tranquil atmosphere with a secluded garden, perfect for enjoying a quiet evening after a day of exploring.

The property's location allows guests to experience both the beach and the countryside, with several walking paths and natural areas nearby. Coastal Cottage is a perfect option for those looking for a peaceful escape in Whitstable while still being within easy reach of the town's attractions.

5. Whitstable Beach House

Whitstable Beach House is a luxurious and spacious rental located right on the edge of Whitstable Beach, offering sweeping views of the estuary. The beach house features stylish, contemporary design, with large windows and an open-plan living area. The property is perfect for large families or groups, offering several bedrooms, a well-equipped kitchen, and ample living space for guests to relax in after a long day.

With direct access to the beach and a short walk to the town center, Whitstable Beach House provides a perfect blend of privacy and convenience. It's an excellent option for visitors who want to enjoy all the beauty and charm of Whitstable while staying in a truly unique, high-end property.

Budget-Friendly Options with Charm

Whitstable's budget-friendly options offer a great mix of charm, comfort, and affordability, making the town accessible to visitors looking for an economical stay without compromising on quality.

1. The Whitstable YHA (Youth Hostel Association)

The Whitstable YHA offers affordable and comfortable accommodation for families, solo travelers, and groups. Located near the seafront, this budget-friendly hostel provides both dormitory-style rooms and private rooms, offering flexibility for a variety of travel styles.

The YHA also has a shared kitchen, which allows guests to save money by preparing their own meals, and a common area for socializing and relaxing.

The location is excellent, with easy access to Whitstable's beach and harbor. The relaxed atmosphere and affordability make it a great option for those traveling on a budget.

2. The Prince of Wales Hotel
The Prince of Wales Hotel is a charming, budget-friendly hotel located in the heart of Whitstable. While not as luxurious as some of the town's boutique hotels, The Prince of Wales offers affordable, well-maintained rooms with comfortable amenities. The hotel has a relaxed pub atmosphere and serves hearty meals, including classic British pub fare.

The Prince of Wales is an excellent choice for visitors who want to enjoy the local experience without breaking the bank. The location is central, providing easy access to Whitstable's main attractions and restaurants.

3. The Oyster Catcher Hostel

Located a little outside of the town center, The Oyster Catcher Hostel provides simple, comfortable accommodations at affordable prices. With shared dorms and private rooms available, this hostel is ideal for those who want to stay near the beach without paying a premium for luxury accommodations. The property offers communal spaces, including a kitchen and lounge area, allowing guests to socialize and enjoy the relaxed Whitstable vibe.

The Oyster Catcher Hostel is a great option for younger travelers or those on a tighter budget, providing a lively atmosphere and easy access to Whitstable's top attractions.

4. Seashells Guest House

Seashells Guest House is a budget-friendly B&B that offers cozy rooms and a welcoming environment. Located near Whitstable's beach, the guest house offers simple yet comfortable rooms, along with a full English breakfast each morning. The friendly owners are always happy to provide recommendations for local restaurants, attractions, and activities.

The affordability, combined with the homely atmosphere and proximity to the beach, makes Seashells Guest House a great option for those looking for a charming and budget-conscious place to stay in Whitstable.

5. The Harbour View Guest House

The Harbour View Guest House offers budget-friendly accommodation with a focus on comfort and convenience. The guest house features light, airy rooms and is located within walking distance of Whitstable's main attractions, including the harbor, beach, and local restaurants. The Harbor View Guest House is ideal for visitors who want to experience the charm of Whitstable without spending a fortune.

Conclusion

Whether you're looking for a luxurious boutique hotel, a cozy beachfront cottage, or a budget-friendly guesthouse, Whitstable offers a wide range of accommodation options that cater to different tastes and budgets. The town's charm, combined with its unique coastal setting, ensures that every stay is an unforgettable experience, whether you're enjoying the modern luxury of a boutique hotel or the peaceful simplicity of a quaint guesthouse by the sea.

CHAPTER SIX: ART, CULTURE, AND CREATIVITY

Whitstable's Galleries and Studios

Whitstable, renowned for its vibrant arts scene, is home to an eclectic mix of galleries and studios that showcase both local talent and national artists. From contemporary exhibitions to traditional art forms, the town offers a rich cultural experience for visitors interested in art and creativity.

1. The Whitstable Biennale

The Whitstable Biennale is one of the town's premier art events, held every two years. This internationally recognized festival celebrates contemporary visual art across a wide range of mediums. The Biennale brings together established and emerging artists from around the world, offering a platform for innovative work that challenges and excites. With installations, performances, and interactive art spaces, the Whitstable Biennale invites visitors to engage with cutting-edge art in an open, community-focused environment.

Exhibitions during the Biennale often take place in various locations around the town, including empty warehouses, public spaces, and outdoor settings, providing an immersive experience that blends the town's natural beauty with avant-garde creativity. The event is a must-visit for anyone passionate about contemporary art.

2. The Horsebridge Arts Centre
A focal point of Whitstable's arts scene, The Horsebridge Arts Centre is a community-run venue that hosts a wide variety of exhibitions, performances, and workshops. Located in the heart of the town, The Horsebridge is a hub for local artists, musicians, and performers. The gallery space frequently exhibits works by Whitstable-based artists, alongside guest artists from further afield.

In addition to visual arts, the center offers music concerts, dance performances, and theater productions, making it a key venue for anyone interested in the creative culture of Whitstable. The space also hosts workshops, where visitors can try their hand at everything from painting to pottery.

3. The Art House Whitstable

The Art House Whitstable is an artist-run space that provides a platform for contemporary visual art. Known for its welcoming and relaxed atmosphere, the gallery showcases a diverse range of exhibitions throughout the year, with a focus on emerging and experimental art forms. The space also hosts art events, such as artist talks, film screenings, and live performances, creating a community of artists and art enthusiasts.

The gallery often offers opportunities for visitors to engage with the art-making process, including hands-on workshops and art classes. The Art House Whitstable is an ideal location for anyone wanting to immerse themselves in the creative energy of the town and explore new forms of artistic expression.

4. Whitstable Gallery

Located in a charming building near the seafront, the Whitstable Gallery is one of the town's most established venues for contemporary art. Featuring a rotating selection of exhibitions, the gallery is known for its impressive collection of paintings, sculptures, and photography, with a particular focus on artists who draw inspiration from the local landscape.

The gallery is committed to showcasing the work of both established and emerging artists, and its exhibits often feature themes tied to the town's natural beauty, maritime heritage, and coastal lifestyle. The Whitstable Gallery also provides a platform for international artists, making it an exciting place to discover new artistic voices.

5. The Harbour Gallery

Situated on the picturesque Whitstable Harbour, The Harbour Gallery is a small but vibrant space showcasing local artwork. It offers a range of original paintings, prints, and sculptures created by local artists, many of whom are inspired by Whitstable's distinctive coastal environment. The gallery's location by the water provides a perfect backdrop for showcasing art inspired by the sea and the changing tides.

The Harbour Gallery is a popular stop for those looking to take home a piece of Whitstable's creative spirit. With its range of affordable artwork and intimate setting, it offers a unique opportunity to connect with the town's artistic community.

6. The Oyster Art Studio
The Oyster Art Studio is a creative space where visitors can explore the work of local artists, from paintings and ceramics to photography and mixed-media pieces. The studio hosts a variety

of exhibitions throughout the year, often focused on themes that resonate with the town's coastal culture. The space also offers workshops and classes, providing an opportunity for visitors to engage directly with the creative process.

This studio is known for its welcoming atmosphere and its dedication to fostering creativity among both professional and amateur artists. The Oyster Art Studio serves as a creative sanctuary, encouraging visitors to explore new forms of artistic expression in a relaxed and supportive environment.

Annual Festivals and Events

Whitstable's cultural calendar is packed with festivals and events that celebrate its artistic heritage and the creative spirit that defines the town. From arts festivals to community gatherings, there is always something happening in Whitstable for those interested in culture and creativity.

1. Whitstable Biennale

As mentioned, the Whitstable Biennale is a major event in the town's cultural calendar, held every two years. It is an important celebration of contemporary art, with exhibitions, installations, and performances happening throughout the town. Artists from all over the world come to Whitstable to showcase their work, and the town transforms into a vibrant art hub for the duration of the event. The Biennale includes outdoor art, gallery exhibitions, site-specific installations, and a series of performances that draw on the town's maritime and cultural heritage.

This event brings together both local residents and international visitors, creating a dynamic space for dialogue, creativity, and artistic exchange. The Whitstable Biennale has become a key event for the arts in Kent and beyond.

2. Whitstable Oyster Festival
The Whitstable Oyster Festival, one of the town's oldest and most beloved events, celebrates the local oyster industry and the town's maritime heritage. The festival includes a

range of activities, such as live music, parades, food stalls, cooking demonstrations, and, of course, the opportunity to taste Whitstable's famous oysters.

The event takes place every summer and has become a significant occasion for both locals and visitors. It highlights the town's close connection to the sea, offering a unique mix of celebration, community spirit, and cultural tradition. The Oyster Festival also features performances by local musicians, dance groups, and other entertainment, making it an exciting and vibrant event for all ages.

3. Whitstable Music Festival
The Whitstable Music Festival is a lively celebration of live music, featuring a diverse range of genres, from jazz and blues to indie and folk. Held annually, the festival attracts musicians and music lovers from across the UK and beyond. Performances take place in various venues around town, including The Horsebridge

Arts Centre, The Marine Hotel, and several outdoor spaces near the beach.

The Whitstable Music Festival provides a platform for both emerging artists and established musicians, with an emphasis on local talent. The festival fosters a sense of community and brings together people of all ages to enjoy the shared experience of live music in the heart of Whitstable.

4. Whitstable Literary Festival
Celebrating the written word, the Whitstable Literary Festival is a must-attend event for book lovers. Held annually, this festival brings together authors, poets, and readers for a weekend of talks, readings, and workshops. The festival often features a blend of well-known authors and emerging voices, with discussions on a wide range of topics, from fiction and poetry to nonfiction and local history.

The Whitstable Literary Festival provides a chance for writers and readers to engage with each other in an intimate and friendly setting. It's a great way to explore the literary landscape of Whitstable and the surrounding areas, while also learning from some of the best authors working today.

5. Artisan and Craft Fairs
Throughout the year, Whitstable hosts a number of artisan and craft fairs, where visitors can purchase unique handmade goods from local artists and craftspeople. These fairs are held in various locations around the town, including the seafront and the Horsebridge Arts Centre, and showcase a wide range of items, including pottery, jewelry, textiles, and fine art.

These fairs provide a wonderful opportunity to explore the creativity of Whitstable's local community, and they are popular with visitors looking for unique, high-quality souvenirs or gifts. Many of the artisans featured in these fairs also offer workshops, allowing visitors to try their hand at various crafts.

Live Music and Local Performances

Whitstable has a lively live music and performance scene, with numerous venues offering regular events that showcase the town's musical talent and vibrant arts culture.

1. The Whitstable Playhouse

The Whitstable Playhouse is the town's main theater venue, hosting a diverse range of performances, including plays, comedy shows, live music, and community events. The Playhouse is known for its warm, welcoming atmosphere and its commitment to providing a platform for local talent. Many performances focus on the work of Kent-based writers, actors, and musicians, but the venue also hosts touring productions and performances from across the UK.

The Whitstable Playhouse is an excellent venue for those looking to enjoy live theater or music in an intimate setting. The space is flexible and can accommodate a wide range of performances, from small-scale plays to large music concerts.

2. The Duke's Head

For a more relaxed live music experience, The Duke's Head, a local pub, offers live music performances most weekends. From acoustic sessions to full band gigs, the pub is a popular spot for music lovers who enjoy a laid-back setting and a lively atmosphere. The Duke's Head features both local musicians and visiting acts, creating a diverse and exciting music scene in Whitstable.

The intimate setting of The Duke's Head allows guests to enjoy high-quality live performances while savoring a drink and socializing with the friendly crowd. The venue is an important part of Whitstable's music scene, providing a place for both established and emerging talent to showcase their work.

3. The Prince of Wales

Another key venue for live music in Whitstable is The Prince of Wales, a traditional pub located near the harbor. The pub hosts live music several nights a week, ranging from folk and blues to rock and jazz. The Prince of Wales is known for its relaxed, welcoming atmosphere, and its live music events are a favorite among locals and visitors alike.

With its cozy interior and excellent acoustics, The Prince of Wales offers an enjoyable setting for those looking to experience live music in Whitstable. The venue is also a great place to meet other music fans and enjoy a pint while taking in a performance.

4. The Crab & Winkle Café
For a more intimate live performance experience, The Crab & Winkle Café regularly hosts acoustic sets, jazz performances, and poetry readings. Located in the heart of Whitstable, this cozy café offers a platform for local musicians and performers to share their talents with a small, appreciative audience. The relaxed ambiance and excellent food make it a great spot to enjoy live music while experiencing Whitstable's creative vibe.

Conclusion

Whitstable's thriving arts, culture, and creative scene is a vital part of the town's identity, attracting artists, musicians, and visitors from across the world. With its diverse galleries, annual festivals, and vibrant live music scene, Whitstable is a place where creativity flourishes and cultural expression is celebrated. Whether you're exploring the contemporary art installations at the Whitstable Biennale, enjoying a live music gig in a local pub, or attending one of the town's many festivals, Whitstable offers a wealth of opportunities to engage with its unique creative spirit.

CHAPTER SEVEN: SHOPPING AND LOCAL TREASURES

Whitstable offers a unique and rewarding shopping experience, where visitors can discover a blend of independent boutiques, vintage finds, artisanal crafts, and handmade goods. The town's local shops reflect its vibrant culture and creative spirit, with many stores offering one-of-a-kind items that can't be found elsewhere. Whether you're in search of a special souvenir or simply want to explore Whitstable's shopping scene, there is something for everyone. Below is a detailed guide to the town's shopping hotspots and treasures you shouldn't miss.

Independent Boutiques and Vintage Finds
Whitstable is known for its charming independent boutiques, each offering a carefully curated selection of clothing, accessories, homeware, and gifts. Many of these boutiques

are family-owned or run by local entrepreneurs, giving them a distinct personality and an emphasis on unique, high-quality products.

1. The Whitstable Clothing Company

For those interested in stylish, locally-inspired clothing, The Whitstable Clothing Company is a must-visit. Specializing in casual, coastal-inspired fashion, the store offers a range of comfortable yet chic clothing, perfect for both a day at the beach and a casual evening out. From nautical-themed sweaters to linen shirts and summer dresses, the boutique features both timeless pieces and trendy styles, often designed with the local coastline in mind. The store also carries a selection of accessories, including scarves, hats, and beach bags, making it an ideal spot for refreshing your wardrobe with pieces that reflect the town's seaside charm.

2. Vintage at the Warehouse

If you're a fan of vintage fashion and unique finds, Vintage at the Warehouse is the place to go. Located in a converted industrial building, this store offers an eclectic mix of retro and vintage clothing, shoes, accessories, and homeware. From classic 1960s dresses to 1980s leather jackets, you'll find a variety of styles and eras represented. The shop's laid-back atmosphere and curated selection make it a great place to discover one-of-a-kind pieces. The team behind the store is knowledgeable and passionate about vintage items, offering advice on how to incorporate timeless pieces into modern outfits.

3. Penny & Ruth's Vintage Emporium

For even more vintage treasures, Penny & Ruth's Vintage Emporium is a charming stop in the heart of Whitstable. This boutique offers a range of antique and vintage clothing, alongside an impressive selection of vintage furniture, home accessories, and retro items. Whether you're on the hunt for a vintage tea set, a statement jacket, or quirky home decor, you'll find a variety of items that reflect Whitstable's love for history and style. The boutique's friendly owners are always happy to share the stories behind the pieces, making the experience both fun and educational.

4. Wild and Wolf

If you're looking for contemporary fashion with a twist, Wild and Wolf is an independent boutique that perfectly blends modern style with artistic flair. Located on the high street, this shop offers a curated selection of unique clothing and accessories, often created by local designers. The boutique also specializes in eco-friendly fashion, featuring sustainable fabrics and ethical fashion brands that focus on reducing their environmental impact. Wild and Wolf is perfect for those who want to support local designers while making eco-conscious fashion choices.

5. The White House

Located on the main high street, The White House is another boutique offering a blend of coastal-inspired fashion and homeware. The store showcases a variety of clothing, jewelry, and gifts with a soft, neutral color palette. Its selection is elegant and simple, featuring designs that evoke the tranquility of Whitstable's seaside atmosphere. The store also carries homeware pieces, including ceramics, throws, and other decorative items, making it an ideal spot for both fashion lovers and those looking to refresh their homes with coastal-inspired touches.

Artisanal Crafts and Handmade Goods

Whitstable is a haven for artisans and craftspeople, and visitors will find a variety of handmade goods and artisanal products in the town's many galleries and shops. The creative spirit of the town is reflected in its craftsmanship, and purchasing locally made goods is a fantastic way to support the town's vibrant arts community.

1. The Whitstable Artisan Market

One of the best places to discover handmade goods and artisanal crafts is the Whitstable Artisan Market, which takes place every month. Held in the heart of the town, this market features a rotating selection of local makers, designers, and artists. From handmade jewelry to organic skincare products and pottery, you'll find a wide range of high-quality items made by local artisans. The market is a great opportunity to purchase something unique and locally produced, whether you're looking for a gift or a personal treat.

2. Basil & Bessie
For beautifully crafted pottery, head to Basil & Bessie, a local ceramics studio that creates stunning, handmade pieces inspired by the natural beauty of Whitstable and its surrounding landscapes. The studio's collection includes functional pottery, such as mugs, bowls, and vases, as well as decorative items, including sculptures and bespoke pieces. Each item is crafted with care and attention to detail, making them perfect for those seeking distinctive, handmade treasures.

3. Stitch and Make
Stitch and Make is a wonderful shop for anyone who appreciates textile arts. Specializing in handmade and vintage-inspired textiles, the store

offers everything from hand-stitched quilts and cushions to handwoven scarves and rugs. Many of the items are created using traditional techniques, and the shop's owner frequently runs workshops where visitors can learn how to make their own creations. For those interested in unique, handcrafted textiles, Stitch and Make offers an exceptional selection of goods that beautifully reflect Whitstable's artisanal charm.

4. Whitstable Glassworks

At Whitstable Glassworks, visitors can discover beautiful handmade glassware and artwork. Specializing in glassblowing and kiln-formed glass techniques, the studio produces a wide range of products, from glass jewelry to large, sculptural pieces. The studio's work often takes inspiration from the sea, with pieces incorporating fluid, organic shapes and colors that reflect Whitstable's coastal beauty. Whitstable Glassworks also offers workshops, where you can try your hand at creating your own glass pieces.

5. The Little Shop of Glass

The Little Shop of Glass is a delightful shop that specializes in both hand-blown glass ornaments and practical glassware. From delicate glass necklaces to decorative glass paperweights, the store's collection reflects the area's maritime influence, with many pieces featuring waves, seascapes, and nautical designs. Whether you're looking for a small gift or a statement piece for your home, the Little Shop of Glass offers beautifully crafted items that showcase the artistry of local glassmakers.

6. Whitstable Candles

For a fragrant and cozy gift, Whitstable Candles offers a stunning selection of handmade, scented candles. Each candle is created using high-quality natural waxes and infused with essential oils, making them both eco-friendly and aromatic. The shop carries a range of scents inspired by the town's coastal environment, from salty sea breeze to floral notes reminiscent of local gardens. These candles make for perfect souvenirs or thoughtful gifts that capture the essence of Whitstable.

What to Buy as a Souvenir

Whitstable offers a variety of unique souvenirs that reflect its coastal charm, artistic spirit, and maritime heritage. Whether you're looking for a keepsake to remember your visit or a gift to bring home to loved ones, there are plenty of options to choose from.

1. Oysters and Oyster-Related Products

Whitstable is famous for its oysters, and you can't leave the town without bringing home some of its signature shellfish. While fresh oysters may be difficult to transport, there are a number of oyster-related products available as souvenirs. Many local shops sell oyster-shaped jewelry, oyster shells for decoration, and oyster-themed homeware. Whitstable also offers gourmet oyster sauces, oyster salts, and even oyster shell-based skincare products, all of which make great gifts or personal treats.

2. Locally Made Art and Prints

For art lovers, one of the best souvenirs to buy in Whitstable is a piece of locally made artwork. Many of the town's galleries and studios sell prints, paintings, and photographs that capture the beauty of Whitstable's seafront, landscapes, and town life. Whether you're looking for a large painting to adorn your home or a small print to remind you of your visit, Whitstable's art scene offers a range of affordable and high-quality options.

3. Local Sea Salt and Gourmet Products

Whitstable's coastal location means that it's home to a number of artisanal food products, and local sea salt is one of the most popular items to bring back as a souvenir. Available in various flavors, from smoked salt to flavored varieties, Whitstable's sea salt is perfect for culinary enthusiasts. Other gourmet products include local honey, jams, and chutneys, all made with ingredients sourced from the surrounding area. These products make great gifts for food lovers or for anyone who appreciates the taste of Kent's countryside and coast.

4. Handmade Jewelry and Accessories
Whitstable is home to many talented jewelers who create beautiful, unique pieces inspired by the town's coastal environment. You'll find a variety of handmade jewelry, from delicate silver earrings featuring sea glass to necklaces made from local pebbles. Many shops also sell accessories like scarves, hats, and bags, which are perfect souvenirs for those who want to take home a piece of Whitstable's creative spirit.

5. Seaside Homeware
For souvenirs that will remind you of Whitstable's coastal charm, consider purchasing seaside-inspired homeware. Many local shops offer items such as nautical-themed cushions, ceramic fish, and coastal-themed decor. These items are perfect for adding a touch of Whitstable's relaxed, beachy vibe to your home, whether you're decorating a seaside cottage or

simply want to remember your trip to this unique town.

Conclusion

Whitstable's shopping scene is a reflection of the town's unique character and creative energy. From independent boutiques offering coastal-inspired fashion to artisanal markets filled with handmade goods, there's no shortage of treasures to discover. Whether you're on the hunt for a vintage find, a one-of-a-kind piece of art, or a souvenir that captures the essence of Whitstable, the town offers a wealth of shopping options that will make your visit memorable. By supporting local businesses and artisans, you'll not only take home something special but also contribute to the vibrant creative community that makes Whitstable such a unique and welcoming destination.

CHAPTER EIGHT: DAY TRIPS AND NEARBY ATTRACTIONS

While Whitstable itself offers an abundance of charm, coastal beauty, and history, the surrounding area is home to some equally exciting destinations that are well worth visiting on a day trip. Whether you're looking to explore ancient cathedrals, visit historic landmarks, or enjoy charming market towns, the areas surrounding Whitstable are packed with attractions that will enrich your trip. Here are some of the best day trips and nearby attractions you should consider when visiting Whitstable.

Canterbury and Its Cathedral

Canterbury, a UNESCO World Heritage site, is one of the most iconic destinations in the United Kingdom. Just a short drive from Whitstable, the city is best known for its stunning cathedral, but it offers much more than just this historic landmark.

1. Canterbury Cathedral

At the heart of Canterbury lies its world-famous cathedral, an architectural masterpiece that dates back to 597 AD. A visit to the cathedral is a must for anyone exploring the area, as it's a significant religious site, a place of pilgrimage, and an iconic symbol of English history. The cathedral is a UNESCO World Heritage site and serves as the seat of the Archbishop of Canterbury, the leader of the Church of England. Visitors can marvel at its incredible Gothic architecture, intricate stained glass windows, and the impressive spires that dominate the skyline.

Inside the cathedral, visitors can explore the crypt, which is home to some of the earliest Christian remains in Britain, and the Quire, with its stunning woodwork and vaulted ceilings. The cathedral also has an impressive collection of relics and memorials, including the tomb of Thomas Becket, the Archbishop of Canterbury who was martyred in 1170. The cathedral grounds are also beautiful, with a tranquil green area and lovely gardens offering a peaceful respite from the bustling city.

2. The Canterbury Roman Museum

For history enthusiasts, the Canterbury Roman Museum is an excellent addition to any visit. The museum is built on the site of a Roman townhouse and provides an engaging insight into the city's Roman history. The exhibits include mosaics, pottery, and artifacts that highlight how the Romans lived in Canterbury, known as Durovernum Cantiacorum during Roman times. One of the standout pieces in the museum is a well-preserved Roman floor mosaic, showcasing the intricate art and craftsmanship of the time.

3. The Canterbury Tales Visitor Attraction

A unique and immersive experience, The Canterbury Tales attraction brings Geoffrey Chaucer's famous literary work to life. Visitors walk through recreations of the scenes described in the book, guided by animatronic characters and a vivid narrative. This interactive experience allows you to step into the world of medieval England and learn about the pilgrims' journey to Canterbury in a fun and engaging way.

4. Westgate Gardens and the River Stour
Westgate Gardens, located near the city center, offers a peaceful green space perfect for a stroll. The gardens are situated along the River Stour, and visitors can enjoy a leisurely walk by the water, or even take a boat trip along the river to see the city from a different perspective. The area is also ideal for picnics, and the garden's mature trees and flower beds create a picturesque setting for a relaxing afternoon.

5. Canterbury's Historic Streets and Shopping
Canterbury's charming streets are lined with a mix of independent shops, cafes, and restaurants, as well as high street stores. The cobbled lanes surrounding the cathedral are home to some of the best boutiques in the region, offering a range of fashion, art, and homeware. The city also

boasts numerous traditional pubs, tea rooms, and eateries where visitors can enjoy local specialties, including freshly made scones with clotted cream and Canterbury lamb.

6. Canterbury Castle
Although much of the castle has been lost to time, the remaining ruins offer a fascinating glimpse into the city's medieval past. The castle, originally built in the 11th century after the Norman Conquest, once stood as an imposing fortress. Today, it serves as a quiet and reflective spot to explore, with views over the city from the top of the motte. The castle site is free to visit, and it's a great place to learn more about the area's history and enjoy some peace and quiet.

Herne Bay and Reculver Towers
Herne Bay, a charming seaside town, is just a short drive from Whitstable, making it a perfect destination for a day trip. Known for its Victorian architecture, scenic seafront, and natural beauty, Herne Bay offers a relaxing and

enjoyable experience. Reculver Towers, just outside of the town, is another must-visit spot for history lovers and nature enthusiasts alike.

1. Herne Bay Seafront and Pier
Herne Bay's seafront is a classic British seaside destination, featuring an iconic pier, pebble beach, and numerous cafes and amusements. The town's historic pier dates back to 1832, making it one of the oldest on the southeast coast. Visitors can enjoy a leisurely stroll along the pier, take in views of the coastline, and stop for a traditional seaside treat such as fish and chips or ice cream.

The beach itself is a perfect spot to relax, with the promenade offering a variety of cafes and shops to explore. You can also visit the Herne Bay Museum and Gallery, which provides insights into the area's history and cultural heritage.

2. Reculver Towers

A short distance from Herne Bay, the Reculver Towers are an iconic landmark that serves as a reminder of the area's rich history. The remains of a Roman fort and medieval church stand proudly at the top of a hill, offering dramatic views of the surrounding coastline. The towers themselves are the remnants of St. Mary's Church, which was built in the 12th century and was later abandoned in the 19th century. The site is rich with history, and visitors can explore the ruins while learning about the site's significance in Roman and medieval times.

The area surrounding Reculver Towers is also a nature reserve, with plenty of walking trails and birdwatching opportunities. The flat landscape is ideal for cycling, and the Reserve is home to a wide variety of wildlife, making it an excellent spot for nature lovers.

3. Herne Bay's Historical Attractions
In addition to its seafront, Herne Bay is home to several historical attractions, including the quaint Victorian buildings in the town center.

Many of the properties along the seafront date back to the 19th century, and a walk through the town provides a glimpse into the area's architectural past. The Herne Bay Heritage Trail takes visitors on a self-guided tour of key landmarks and is an excellent way to explore the town's rich history.

4. Reculver Country Park and Beach

Reculver Country Park is a peaceful green space that offers stunning views of the sea and the Reculver Towers. It's a great place for a picnic, a walk, or a quiet afternoon. The park is also home to a variety of birdlife and wildlife, making it a popular spot for nature enthusiasts. The park leads directly to the beach, where you can enjoy a peaceful walk along the coast, far from the crowds of other popular seaside towns.

Faversham's Markets and Breweries

Faversham, another gem in Kent, is an ancient market town that combines history with a thriving arts and food scene. Just a short drive from Whitstable, Faversham is known for its historic markets, beautiful architecture, and strong links to local brewing traditions.

1. Faversham Market

Faversham's bustling market is one of the oldest in England, dating back to the 13th century. Held every Tuesday, Friday, and Saturday, the market offers a fantastic selection of local produce, crafts, antiques, and vintage items. Farmers' market stalls sell fresh, seasonal produce, while you can also find artisanal cheeses, meats, and baked goods from local producers. Faversham's market is an ideal destination for foodies and those looking to take home some authentic Kentish produce.

The market is set in the heart of Faversham, just a short walk from the town's historic High Street. The lively atmosphere and friendly traders make it a wonderful place to experience local life, and it's an excellent spot to pick up unique gifts and souvenirs.

2. Faversham's Historic High Street

Faversham's High Street is lined with beautiful historic buildings, including timber-framed houses, old coaching inns, and listed landmarks. The town is rich in history, and visitors can spend hours wandering through its cobbled streets, discovering independent shops, cafes, and historic pubs. The Shepherd Neame Brewery, the oldest brewery in England, is located near the High Street and is worth a visit for beer lovers.

3. Shepherd Neame Brewery Tour
Founded in 1698, Shepherd Neame Brewery is one of the oldest and most famous breweries in the country. The brewery offers guided tours that take visitors through its brewing process, from the malting of the barley to the final bottling of the beer. The tour also includes tastings of the brewery's award-winning beers, including the iconic Spitfire Ale, named after the famous fighter plane. The brewery tour is an informative and enjoyable experience, providing a fascinating glimpse into Kent's rich brewing history.

4. Faversham Creek and the Shipyard

Faversham Creek is another notable feature of the town, offering scenic views and opportunities for a leisurely walk. The creek has historically been a hub for shipbuilding, and some of the old shipyards are still operational today. The area is a lovely spot for a stroll, with quaint riverside cafes and beautiful views over the water.

5. Faversham's Historic Pubs and Restaurants

Faversham also has a great selection of pubs and restaurants that highlight local produce and traditional British cuisine. Many of the town's pubs have a long history, with some dating back centuries. A visit to one of Faversham's historic inns or traditional pubs is a perfect way to enjoy the local atmosphere and unwind after a day of exploring.

Conclusion

The areas surrounding Whitstable are rich in history, culture, and natural beauty, making them perfect for day trips. Whether you're drawn to the ancient history and stunning architecture of Canterbury, the seaside charm and historic landmarks of Herne Bay, or the market-town vibes and brewing heritage of Faversham, these nearby attractions offer something for every traveler. Each destination is easily accessible from Whitstable, making them ideal for exploring on a day trip, and they promise to enhance your overall experience of this beautiful corner of Kent.

CHAPTER NINE: INSIDER TIPS AND LOCAL ETIQUETTE

Whitstable, a charming seaside town in Kent, offers visitors a perfect blend of traditional British coastal beauty and a vibrant, artistic atmosphere. While the town is relatively small, it attracts a steady flow of tourists, particularly during the summer months. If you're looking to enjoy the town to its fullest, here are insider tips and local etiquette to ensure a smooth, enjoyable visit, while blending in like a local and respecting the town's values.

Best Times to Visit and Avoid Crowds
Whitstable is a popular destination, particularly during the summer, when tourists flock to enjoy its beaches, seafood, and coastal charm. However, for those seeking a quieter experience or aiming to avoid large crowds, the timing of your visit is key.

1. Visit During the Shoulder Seasons:

Spring (April to early June): This is perhaps the best time to visit Whitstable. The town comes alive with blooming flowers, outdoor events, and mild weather, but without the overwhelming crowds of the summer. The beaches are quieter, the town's shops and cafes are more relaxed, and you'll have the chance to enjoy the early season's produce, like freshly caught oysters and local vegetables.

Autumn (September to early November): Early autumn is another great time to visit. The summer tourists have mostly returned home, but the weather is still pleasant for outdoor activities. The autumn months also offer the opportunity to sample seasonal produce and enjoy festivals like the Whitstable Oyster Festival, which typically occurs in late July, but the town remains calm and welcoming through September.

2. Avoiding the Peak Summer Months:

July and August: These are the peak months for tourism in Whitstable, especially around the Oyster Festival. While these months are full of events and life, they also come with crowded streets, higher accommodation prices, and bustling beaches. If you don't mind the hustle and bustle and love being part of a lively scene, then this is the time for you, but for those looking for tranquility, it's best to avoid this peak period.

3. Weather Considerations:

Winter (December to February): While it's not peak season, Whitstable's winter months are a great time to experience the town in a different light. Fewer tourists mean fewer queues and a peaceful atmosphere, perfect for enjoying the town's pubs and coastal walks. While some businesses may close for the season or have reduced hours, many still operate and offer a welcoming experience. However, the weather can be quite chilly, so packing warm clothes is a must.

Spring and Autumn Weather: Both seasons generally offer mild temperatures, with rain being a possibility, so packing layers and a waterproof jacket is recommended. The unpredictable nature of British weather can sometimes make it difficult to plan outdoor activities, so it's wise to check forecasts in advance.

How to Blend In Like a Local
Whitstable has a distinct local culture, with a mix of fishermen, creatives, and long-time residents. While it's welcoming to tourists, understanding the local customs and how to act like a local can enhance your experience and make you feel more integrated into the community.

1. Respect Local Traditions and the Town's Pace:

Whitstable has a relaxed, easy-going vibe, and the locals pride themselves on enjoying a slower pace of life compared to busy city living. Visitors should follow this relaxed attitude by not rushing around too much and enjoying the laid-back atmosphere.

Take your time at cafés: Locals love to sit in cafés for hours, sipping coffee or enjoying a leisurely lunch. Don't rush your meal or coffee; it's part of the local lifestyle. Also, avoid rushing service staff—many establishments work at a more relaxed pace compared to big cities.

Enjoy leisurely walks: Whitstable's charm is best experienced on foot. Instead of speeding through, take time to walk around the town, explore its streets, and stop at its little boutiques and art galleries. Locals often spend time strolling along the beach or the High Street, so joining them for a gentle wander is a great way to experience the town.

2. Embrace Local Food Culture:

Try the local seafood: The town's most famous delicacy is its oysters. When in Whitstable, it's a must to try oysters at one of the local oyster bars or seafood restaurants. Locals often enjoy oysters with a squeeze of lemon or a dollop of tabasco sauce, and you should follow suit when visiting these establishments. If you're unfamiliar with oysters, don't hesitate to ask your server for tips on how to eat them.

Order drinks like a local: When it comes to pubs, beer is typically a favorite drink for the locals, especially the traditional ales brewed in Kent. Try a pint of local beer, such as Shepherd Neame's Spitfire Ale, which is a local staple. Locals tend to prefer their drinks served in traditional pint glasses, so avoid ordering "larger" than necessary if you're unfamiliar with pub etiquette.

Respect for food waste: Locals are generally quite mindful of food waste, and many businesses in Whitstable pride themselves on serving fresh and local food. Be mindful of portion sizes and try to finish what you order, or be sure to ask for a smaller serving if you're unsure.

3. Local Interaction and Small Talk:

The local accent and politeness: The Kentish accent is soft and approachable, and locals are known for being friendly and polite. When you interact with people, greeting them with a simple "hello" or "good morning" is expected. Small talk is common, particularly with shopkeepers or in cafés. Locals enjoy talking about the weather, the day's news, or any of the town's events, so don't be afraid to engage in these casual conversations.

No need for formalities: While you may be tempted to call people "sir" or "madam," locals prefer a more relaxed approach. Just using a friendly "excuse me" or "please" is typically sufficient. When it comes to dining, it's customary to refer to your waiter or waitress by their first name if they introduce themselves, but addressing them as "sir" or "madam" can feel too formal in this friendly environment.

Respect the quiet: Whitstable is a community that values peace and quiet, especially in residential areas. When walking through quieter streets or by the beach, keep noise to a minimum, avoid loud music, and respect the private nature of the town's more residential areas.

4. Participate in Local Events and Festivals:

Join the Oyster Festival: The Whitstable Oyster Festival is one of the biggest local events, celebrating the town's famous seafood. While many tourists attend, locals take part in the parade, enjoy live music, and participate in competitions. If you're visiting in July, consider taking part in the festival, which showcases the local culture and gives you a deeper understanding of the town's ties to the sea.

Art and Culture Events: Whitstable has a rich arts scene, with regular art exhibitions, local performances, and pop-up galleries. It's not uncommon to see an impromptu gallery or live music performance in a local café or pub. If you're in town during a cultural event, such as Whitstable's Arts Festival or Open Studios event, immerse yourself in the local creative scene.

Safety, Sustainability, and Travel Etiquette
Whitstable takes pride in its coastal environment and community, and visitors are encouraged to respect both. Safety is a priority, as well as sustainable travel practices that help preserve the town's charm.

1. Safety Tips for Visiting Whitstable:

Pedestrian Awareness: Whitstable is a pedestrian-friendly town, but with narrow roads and busy streets, it's important to be mindful of traffic. Always use designated crosswalks when crossing streets, and keep an eye out for cyclists, who often use the same lanes as cars. Additionally, during busy summer months, streets can get crowded, so it's a good idea to keep your belongings close and watch out for pickpockets in crowded areas.

Beach Safety: Whitstable's beaches are generally safe for swimming, but it's important to follow local advice regarding water conditions. Pay attention to any signage about swimming safety and be aware of tides and currents. Lifeguards are on duty during peak seasons, but you should always swim with caution, especially when visiting the less-patrolled areas.

Emergency Services: Whitstable is a small town, but emergency services are available if needed. The local police station is located in the center of town, and there are several hospitals and urgent care centers nearby in Canterbury.

2. Sustainability and Respecting the Environment:

Sustainable Practices: Whitstable's residents are increasingly committed to sustainability, and it's important to respect this ethos while visiting. Be mindful of littering by disposing of trash responsibly and using the recycling bins available throughout the town. Many local businesses actively promote eco-friendly practices, such as using biodegradable packaging, so consider supporting these establishments.

Respecting Wildlife: Whitstable is home to various wildlife, including seabirds and marine life. If you're taking part in outdoor activities such as walking along the coast or participating in water sports, avoid disturbing wildlife. Keep your distance from birds and other animals, and ensure your actions don't harm the environment.

3. General Travel Etiquette:

Tip Generously: In the UK, tipping is not mandatory, but it is appreciated for good service.

In restaurants, it's common to leave a 10-15% tip for service, especially if the service charge is not already included. In pubs, tipping is usually not required, but if you're ordering at the bar, leaving a small tip for good service is always appreciated.

Mind the Quiet Hours: In the evenings, particularly during the off-season, Whitstable is a peaceful town. While pubs and restaurants will be lively, avoid making excessive noise in residential areas after dark. The town's emphasis on quiet living means that respecting local noise ordinances is key.

Conclusion

Visiting Whitstable can be a memorable and rewarding experience if you follow the local customs and etiquette. Embrace the slow pace of life, take the time to appreciate the town's natural beauty and artistic scene, and respect the community's values of sustainability and friendliness. With the right approach, you'll not only enjoy the sights and sounds of Whitstable but also become a part of its welcoming local atmosphere. Whether you're visiting during the peak summer months or the quieter off-season, following these insider tips will help you make the most of your stay while blending in seamlessly with the locals.

CHAPTER TEN: CONCLUSION: YOUR WHITSTABLE ADVENTURE AWAITS

Whitstable offers visitors a unique blend of natural beauty, artistic creativity, and local charm that guarantees an unforgettable coastal experience. From its iconic oyster bars and scenic beaches to its welcoming local culture, the town promises something for everyone. Whether you are an avid foodie, an art lover, a nature enthusiast, or simply in search of a relaxing getaway, Whitstable offers a diverse range of activities and attractions. Below is your guide to ensuring your trip to Whitstable is well-planned and truly enjoyable.

Trip Planning Checklist
To help you prepare for your adventure, here's a comprehensive trip planning checklist covering

all the essential aspects of your visit to Whitstable. Following this guide will ensure you make the most of your time in this delightful seaside town.

1. Accommodation Arrangements:

Research Accommodation Options: Whitstable offers a range of places to stay, including boutique hotels, charming bed-and-breakfasts, beachfront cottages, and budget-friendly hostels. Depending on your preferences and budget, you can choose from the more luxurious options or opt for a cozy, budget-conscious retreat.

Book Early for Peak Seasons: If you are planning to visit during peak tourist seasons (June-August), it's crucial to book your accommodation well in advance. The town can get busy, and last-minute bookings may leave you with limited options.

Consider Location: Whether you want to stay near the beach, in the heart of the town, or near quieter areas, make sure to choose accommodation based on your preferences. Being close to key attractions, such as Whitstable Harbour or Tankerton Slopes, will enhance your overall experience.

2. Transportation and Getting Around:

Arriving in Whitstable:

By Train: Whitstable is easily accessible by train from London, with direct routes from London Victoria or London St Pancras. The journey takes about 1 to 1.5 hours.
By Car: For those driving, Whitstable is well-connected by the A299, and there's plenty of parking in and around the town.
By Bus: Public buses run frequently between Whitstable and nearby towns, including Canterbury, Herne Bay, and Faversham. Check the schedules to plan your route.

Local Transportation: Once in Whitstable, getting around is easy. The town is small enough to explore on foot or by bike, but you can also rent a car for excursions or day trips to nearby attractions.

3. Packing Essentials:

Clothing for All Seasons: Whitstable's weather can be unpredictable, so pack layers, a light waterproof jacket, and comfortable walking shoes for outdoor exploration. Don't forget sun protection (hat, sunglasses, sunscreen) during the summer.

Swimwear: If you plan to visit the beach, don't forget your swimsuit, beach towels, and a pair of flip-flops for comfort.

Reusable Water Bottle and Eco-Friendly Products: In line with the town's sustainability ethos, pack a reusable water bottle to stay hydrated, as well as eco-friendly items to reduce waste.

Sunscreen and Bug Repellent: Especially if you're hiking or spending time near the water, sunscreen is essential. Bug repellent can also be useful in certain areas, particularly during the warmer months.

4. Plan Your Budget:

Accommodation Costs: Whitstable offers a range of price points, so set a realistic budget based on your accommodation choices. Expect to pay more during peak seasons.

Dining Costs: Eating out in Whitstable is generally affordable, but some premium restaurants and seafood spots can be pricier. Plan a daily food budget and explore both high-end seafood restaurants and casual dining options.

Activities and Excursions: Whether you're booking a sailing trip, renting a bike, or attending an event like the Oyster Festival, factor in activity costs. Many of Whitstable's best attractions, such as the beaches and coastal walks, are free, but special events or guided tours may charge a fee.

5. Health and Safety:

Travel Insurance: Always ensure that you have travel insurance that covers potential cancellations, health emergencies, or lost belongings.

Emergency Numbers: In case of emergency, dial 999 for police, fire, or ambulance services. Familiarize yourself with the locations of the nearest pharmacies, and be sure to have necessary medications or prescriptions.

Stay Hydrated and Healthy: Whitstable is a small town, but with many walking opportunities, staying hydrated and taking breaks as needed is key to enjoying the sights.

Summary of Must-See Highlights

Whitstable's charm lies in its combination of vibrant local culture, stunning natural scenery, and a range of attractions suitable for all types of travelers. Here's a recap of the must-see highlights to ensure you don't miss the best of what the town has to offer:

1. Whitstable Harbour and Harbour Market: Whitstable Harbour is the heart of the town, where visitors can watch boats come and go, explore the fish market, or simply enjoy the views of the sea. The Harbour Market is an eclectic spot, offering a mix of food stalls, local crafts, and artisan products. It's a great place to spend an afternoon sampling local treats like fresh oysters, or simply browsing for souvenirs.

2. The Famous Oyster Experience:

■ Whitstable is world-renowned for its oysters, and no visit is complete without tasting them. Whether at a local seafood restaurant or an oyster bar along the beach, Whitstable's oysters are a must-try. Local establishments like The Oyster Bar or Harbour Street Café are perfect spots to enjoy freshly shucked oysters while enjoying views of the sea.

3. Tankerton Slopes and Beach Huts:

■ For a quintessential British seaside experience, Tankerton Slopes is the perfect place to relax. The sloping grass banks offer stunning views over the sea, and the iconic beach huts are perfect for a photo opportunity. The area is also ideal for picnics, kite flying, or a leisurely stroll along the coast.

4. Whitstable Castle and Gardens:

■ Situated in a beautifully landscaped garden, Whitstable Castle offers a glimpse into the town's history. You can wander through its gardens or enjoy afternoon tea at the café within the castle grounds. The castle is a great spot for a relaxing day, surrounded by flowers and greenery.

5. The Crab and Winkle Way:

■ This former railway track is now a scenic walking and cycling route stretching between Whitstable and Canterbury. The path offers beautiful views of the Kentish countryside, marshes, and woodlands. Ideal for outdoor enthusiasts, the trail is rich in nature and history.

6. Art Galleries and Creative Spaces:

■ Whitstable's thriving arts scene includes a number of galleries, studios, and creative spaces. The Whitstable Biennale is a popular event showcasing contemporary art, and local galleries like The Fish Slab Gallery provide an opportunity to explore local artwork and craftsmanship.

7. The Whitstable Oyster Festival:

■ This annual event, typically held in late July, celebrates the town's oyster heritage with street food, live music, arts and crafts, and more. It's a chance to dive into Whitstable's maritime history, taste oysters, and join in the lively celebrations.

8. The Town's Beaches and Coastal Walks:
■ Whitstable's beaches are among its biggest attractions. From the pebbled beach near the town center to the sandy stretches at Tankerton, there are plenty of spots to relax by the sea. Take a walk along the North Sea coastal path or enjoy

the gentle walk to Reculver Towers, a great spot to witness stunning views over the water.

Final Thoughts and Farewell
Whitstable offers a refreshing and authentic experience for anyone looking to immerse themselves in the beauty of the Kent coast. From its historic harbor and iconic oyster bars to its artistic flair and laid-back lifestyle, the town combines history, nature, and culture into a perfect getaway destination.

By following the tips outlined above, you'll ensure a smooth trip from start to finish. Whether you're here for a weekend or a longer stay, Whitstable's small-town charm and warm hospitality will make your visit unforgettable. With its inviting atmosphere, picturesque views, and creative spirit, Whitstable truly offers an adventure waiting to be explored.

Enjoy your time in Whitstable, and make sure to return again and again to discover more about this delightful seaside gem.

Printed in Dunstable, United Kingdom